DIVORCE OF THE

LEFT & RIGHT

DIVORCE OF THE

LEFT & RIGHT

A COLLECTION OF POETIC WRITING

AMS GOLDEN

Columbus, Ohio

Divorce of the Left & Right

Published by Gatekeeper Press
2167 Stringtown Rd, Suite 109
Columbus, OH 43123-2989
www.GatekeeperPress.com

The cover design for this book is entirely the product of the author. Gatekeeper Press did not participate in and is not responsible for any aspect of this element.

Cover art by AMS Golden. ©2021

Library of Congress Control Number: 2022934703

ISBN (paperback): 9781662913433
eISBN: 9781662918612

To All Who Made This Possible...
Thank you from the bottom of my heart. I must, in part, dedicate this book to you, for without you and your support, motivation, purchases, reviews and commentary, this second book would not have happened. So, thank you. Thank you. Thank you.

Marie T-M
Vincent M
Stefanny & Rachael R
Inez T
Kaitlyn M
Meggie DV
Andrew K
Patricia W-H
Tim C
Sandy D
Jordan F & Llane H
John B
Alessandra M
Kasia N
John G
Maggie S
Alyssa B
Kathleen R
Henry E
Samantha T
Amanda H
Nancy K
Mary Jane S
Betty Z
Bethany S
Stephanie S-D
Mary Beth & Bill G
Denise H
Brianna D-F
Rebecca H

Deborah C
Jared K
Brenda & Michael K
Samantha F
Amanda T
Dana M-N
Dawn P-C
Megan P-H
Suzanne EG-M
Tessa F-MP
Theresa M
Margaret M
Anthony G
William C
Victoria G
Megan M
Tara C
Caitlin C
Eunice Sooyoung K-P
Cristhian A

Promotional Thank Yous
Sandra Dear &
The Little Boho Bookshop

@thereadera
@bookreadersclub
@bookie_mnstr

@rubyisreading_
@simranreadsitall
Beth S
Nicole S
Ricky R
Michelle B
Crystal I
Jodena P
Jessica B
Molly S
Amanda A
Jaida MD
Isabella S
Sarah P
Liam S
Adam C
Anjali M
Sam S
Sarah D-S
Kristin K
Nidhi S
Sally M
Kassandra V
Vanessa T
Angel W
Susan Z
Ciera O
Jessica LG
Becky K
Aurelia L

I also want to take a moment to give a *very* special thank you to...
My Mom & Dad—the best role-models and motivators
My Beautiful Sisters
My Incredible Husband, William Golden
My Real Left and Right Brain, Juliana M. & Tobias H.

Special Book Dedication

Pop & Auntie—Thank you for always supporting me, watching me grow and coming to every little event at school, no matter how small. Thank you for always being my reason to *believe* and motivating me to succeed (no matter how many times I may falter first). You were two of my favorite people, and every day I miss you more. I love you both endlessly and hope that wherever you are, you can see me now, and that I have made you proud.

Contents

The Beginning of the Struggling Artist

Poetry is funny. Some days you write for hours. Some weeks you don't write at all. In those days of empty notebooks, you doubt your potential to ever create more. And people say "it'll just pop into your head." They say "you'll just feel it when you do." But which is it? Because my brain and my heart don't work well together. I'm not sure of what to do. How will I succeed if I don't know where to start?

How will I know if anyone will think my story is "art?"

"Who Are You?"[1]

When I was a little girl I used to smile so often, teachers would pair me up with every student in the class. I guess they thought a smiling child meant a happy child, a successful child. I remember playing with friends using my first tea set... I haven't been invited to a tea party in years. Maybe because last time I let my cups overflow, I spilled tea where no one was ready to clean up such a mess. Hot water burns, it leaves a scar. It's funny how over time the Cheshire Cat became the Mad Hatter... Both smile so cynically, maniacally, but only one carries the weight of "being crazy." If I followed the White Rabbit today, where would he lead me? I'm going to land myself in the hole, right next to Alice. I'm a liability and no one wants to pay my bail. There is no White Rabbit to lead me out. He had to run and I was too late to stay on his course. Instead, I march along with the March Hare; my ability to reason has long deceived me. I drink the poison willingly, like the tag on the bottle says: "Just for you." Grow larger and overwhelm, or smaller and never be enough? I'll be a problem either way. Let the Red Queen shout to her minions, "Off with her head!" A little less weight on my body might make me an attractive prize. A little less brains and I won't be so mad.

Behead me, my Queen. Paint it all red with my blood. Bury me with the last of the white roses. Tell the Morning Glory I said goodnight.

Underdeveloped

I was born nearly two months early, prematurely. My lungs were underdeveloped and they rushed me from my mommy. Psychology might say that's where my ability to form attachments frayed. Could it then explain why I feel like I can never breathe? Or is that just basic biology?

Grow Like a Weed: Wild and Free, Even Where You Shouldn't Be

When we were together you took my voice and made me small.
A child three years old made better conversation than me.
A dog expressed its pain more eloquently.
I always said I wouldn't be "that woman,"
Until it happened and I suddenly gave excuses as reasons.
Three years later I woke up one morning and something had shifted.
I decided you couldn't dust me under the rug—I still existed.
I found my voice, I shouted out loud; most importantly...

I persisted.

Self-Denial

I think I've been choosing second-best all my life because
I was always so sure I'd never get the chance again,
That nothing better could come my way,
That I wasn't worth opportunities or "something special,"
So, I've always jumped at the first "best thing,"
And now everywhere I go, I'm seeing better and yet I never
feel better,
Because I can't bring myself to reach for it,
Because I settled to choose mediocre to keep as "forever,"
Because when you can't see your worth, how can you make
anyone else?

The Left is Right and the Right is Wrong Part 3

The Right is still picking up the broken fragments of you in attempts to create that mosaic you were destined, in her mind, to be. The Left hands her a dustpan and broom and tells her that it's time to stop cutting her fingers on someone who was never real.

The Right begins to sob as The Left says the puzzle she started was always complete—she will never fill in the missing piece.

Not All Idols Are American

How do you do it?
Walk away after swearing to me that you want to stay. And
I still wait for you to come back.
How do you do it?
Tell me how you want to be part of my happiness and then
disappear at my loneliest. And I still make time for you.
How do you do it?
Say you care about me more than anything, and then twist the
knife until I'm sore. And I still tend to your wounds.
How do you do it?
I want to know how you still hold me in your grasp. I want to
have the power that you do. Just look at me. I could be anywhere
right now and I still choose to be in my head because...

It's the only place I'm still with you.

Our Fuse is Out

Our love is like a string of Christmas lights: bright, hopeful, symbolic of joy and happiness...
But our strand has a flaw. A single bulb blown out and only we know. We've buried it at the back of the tree so nobody but us can see.
Our love looks bright, hopeful, symbolic of joy and happiness...
Because no one sees the dark spot we hide from gawking eyes.

Words Can Be Weapons

Whether sent through the wires or spoken out loud,
Either way, you can't white it out.

Think about your words...

Beyond This Poem

It shouldn't matter to me what you think of what I do.
You're out of my life and I haven't even missed you.
But after the years I was your only genuine support in grade
school,
Or how I still have origami notes saved with "don't show or
tell anyone" in your pink pen,
And seeing your growth and your ability to thrive...
Then seeing how easy it was to toss me to the wayside...
Well,
It means way more than it should that you "liked" what you saw—
To reach someone like you motivates me to write more.

Introreflection

Last night I woke up from a dream of you and me. You were so close and yet so far, like we were on two separate lands. I reached across the bed to touch you and you crumbled like sand. Tidal wave after tidal wave of emotion hit the shores of my bed. I scrambled to put you back together, my hands touching fine-grain pieces where you laid. The heat from the friction, the pace at which I worked to keep you from washing away in my memory, molded you into glass. When I came to, I was looking at my reflection, and for once I think I saw myself like you do.

I Am the Reason My Parents are Getting Divorced

The Right and The Left keep fighting over what to do about you.

They don't like when I use their first names—"It's not respectful..." I hear them say. But I haven't felt close to them in years. I've only been able to feel you.

You see, Mom is like me, all heart, and is always crying and hiding in her room. She tells me she hopes I grow stronger and harder than her, but she doesn't realize that if she'd just stand up and take a deep breath, her lungs would flood with oxygen instead of being crippled by her unsaid words.

She thinks you deserve the chance to prove yourself good enough for her baby, and fights to let me see you even after everything we've gone through. Because, she says, "Love is love" and "You deserve to be happy." I don't know how to tell her I'm not sure I'm happy with you anymore, because I'm afraid she likes you more than she ever liked me...

But Dad doesn't like you. *At all.* He says you'll never be good enough for his kid. Tells me to stop seeing you and to cut you off "right now." It's only then that I realize I'm not ready to live without you. So, I tell Dad it's over and he slaps me on the shoulder and says, "Atta boy!" and walks away, unaware that Mom and I just dropped you off at home and I still gave you a kiss goodbye.

But Friday night when I'm running down the stairs and asking to borrow the car, Dad knows... He gives mom *that look* and suddenly I don't know if I'm more grateful to be leaving home, or guilty because I'm not sticking around anymore to watch them feud.

The Left is right—You're no good for me. But with you is the only time I feel anything anymore.

The Right is wrong—I shouldn't have to lie about you anymore. But I don't know how anyone will ever understand this.

And honestly, I don't think my parents will ever be happy again as long as I'm still living in their house...

Dissonance

I sometimes wonder if you chose to love me intentionally because from almost four thousand miles away you felt you were safe from all that comes from being in a lover's presence.

Maybe I Shouldn't Have Put the Calendar Up So Early

The numbers are the only things changing as the years go by.
Age. Date. Time.
And yet nothing is any different. Me. You. Us.

> *How does time keep moving and*
> *still stand completely still?*

Pretty Smiles Hide Ugly Truths

Her heart is open, broken on the floor.
Her eyes have gone blind; she can't hear anymore.
Every day she lives like a child playing pretend.
To stay numb to it all, her senses have all come to an end.
Ask her if she's happy and she will look down and sigh.
If you just ask her if she's happy, she'll break down and cry.

I'll Convince Her

You smell of potential and stale cigarettes.
My mother would only be pleased with one of these. She'll ask you what you do in life and how you plan to provide for me. You'll nervously reply in Lloyd Dobler style, "I know that I don't know... What I really want to do with my life is I want to be with your daughter." And it won't be enough for the woman who believes I deserve more than I could receive in an eternity. But it's enough for me.
See, I believed I deserved my mind's slow torture and being buried alive. I believed I should be pushed from a speeding car and then scolded for not falling quite right. I believed I deserved the abuse of ex-lovers and all the cruel words classmates and "friends" once said. So...
For you to just want to be with me, despite the darkness in my head, means more to me than anything your money could ever buy in the end.

Last Meal

I want to be your favorite dessert; want you to peel me open and dive inside. I promise to quench your thirst. I'll be the sweetest taste on earth...

Weary Night Wears

I do my best writing in the dark hours of morning, the time
when most starving artists are still mourning: lost potential,
failed art, lost lovers, failed start, lost passion, failed sleep, lost
money... Life's not cheap. We starve just to eat.

I guess it's good that the night takes care to shroud us all in
black; otherwise we'd be late looking for appropriate clothes
to wear to our own funerals when our heartaches become
heart attacks.

Do You Love Me Enough to Miss Me?

If I died today,
Tomorrow,
Had it been last night...
Would you cry at my funeral?
Would a piece of you die?

The Battle of Corpus Callosotomy

There's been a civil war in my body since grade seven. The Heart wants control while the Left Brain and Right Brain shout back and forth over its emancipation. "A more perfect Union" is a dream I can't reach. See, I don't even recall anymore how to sleep.

An emotional leader, like Heart, is no match for Left Brain's war-time rhetoric. And the Right Brain wants to run and hide—find attics and closets to wait out the indifference. But Heart is her baby and he needs her protection, so she steps outside to give her dissidence. But then Left Brain is her partner and he needs her full support. They can't let Heart's rebellious angst tear them both apart.

Cerebral fluids, like oceans of alcohol, pull her down and numb her pain. She's so used to being kicked around, she doesn't even realize she's sinking into her grave.

It's dawn and there are battle cries in the bedroom, the kitchen, the den... She wishes she could say they woke her, but she never went to bed.

Shots fired.

She's been hit. In her last gasping breath, she asks her other half to trust their Heart, but he just shakes his head. "This is war, crazy woman," he says before leaving her for dead. Confetti that once was Heart's love manifesto coat the floor she lies on. Her hemorrhaging over his pages makes his work more avant-garde.

Shots fired.

The Heart is hit. He gets so messy, spewing blood where he's been hurt. He raises his weapon in a last attempt to create change and rebirth.

Left Brain shuts down and the silent waves calm him into realizing he'll be dead. The mutual silence on both sides stills the war inside my head. Heart and Left brain had asked which side I would serve on in the end. But I don't know if I will ever be the one that I defend.

Heart?

Brain?

Is it too late to dodge the draft?

It Takes Two

After everyone leaves the party, in the new darkness of the living room, I dance with the ghost of the girl I once was and the girl you once loved. Some days we are one and the same. Some days I am tangoing with a corpse. But every day I'm finding my footing while you're still standing there with two left feet.

This room was meant for living in.

Conversion Therapy

Should this all end tomorrow, I want you to know, you made
an atheist believe in blessings.

There's no other way to explain you...

Even Heroes Get Depressed— and That's Okay!

You don't need to be a hero to be okay.
Get up out of bed today.
Wrap that sheet around your shoulders.
Imagine a red "S."
Now, soar, superhuman.
It's never too late to choose to save yourself.

You've got this. I believe in you.

I Think I Finally Comprehend Miley Cyrus

Let me explain.

I may not have ever traveled to the warmth of Malibu with you, but I can taste it in my coffee, and wouldn't I be damned if the warmth of alcohol and coffee don't make my insides crawl like the warmth you once offered me.

See, I can't be tamed either, and I know, I know you wanted to lasso me in and put me in the stable. You wanted to give me a home to fit in and maybe I'd become more stable. But no. That's not how it works.

See, in 2010 I was in my first downward spiral, and Nine Inch Nails could've never predicted all that could've been when on September 30, 2013, your birthday, Miley Cyrus dropped the album that was my anthem for years to follow. Because, well, they were "bangerz."

See, it was only today when we ended things, and I found myself sipping on Malibu when I realized I understood the broken-hearted lover's evolution: Miley's revolution, because she was never done evolving, she was still resolving problems inside her that hindered her love, and I'd be damned if I didn't admit I had them too.

See, I had no intention of falling in love with you the day that album dropped, but once it was on the charts I knew I wanted us. And that is where the ending starts.

See, we've been dying since the day we were born, ironically because there was too much room to breathe. We were four thousand miles of distance and in years never came to be.

Back then I came in like a wrecking ball because I thought you wanted me to. I came in like a wrecking ball because I absolutely adored you. I came in like a wrecking ball because I just wanted you to let me in.

See, I woke up today after already waking from my nightmares, and realized we are in two different places. I woke up today after I'd already gotten out of bed and brushed my teeth and realized that we didn't reside in the same room in my heart anymore.

See, I grew tired of missing you when you were right there. I grew tired of not sleeping because I was afraid of waking up to what we have become.

When Miley Cyrus wrote *Younger Now*, the album, she was still on a rollercoaster of a ride and Malibu was wishful thinking. But that bad mood, that pain, that resentment... I get it. I, too, know what it's like to be held together by a string.

See, I once thought that string was a red thread of divinity. I thought the universe had this eternal, infinite plan designed for us to meet.

See, I thought you were my soulmate.

But when Miley Cyrus had dropped her sixth album she was seen as eccentric, losing it, out of touch, and I'll be damned if I don't admit I kind of thought so, too. But let me tell you, *now* I get it.

See, I've cut and colored my hair. I'll get married one day thinking it will solve my feelings of loneliness; make me feel like I could be loved. I put myself in hot water so many times, it's amazing I still have skin.

See, maybe I'm just crazy, but I get why she seemed so out of control. Because wild horses are meant to run free, but even wild horses need to feel like they have a haven to run to. And when you find someone who takes the rope from your neck and guides you home, you don't want to believe it's true. Because it's *got* to be too good to be true. I get her when she says she gets so scared of what she can't understand.

See, I don't understand this. I don't understand you. You frighten me. You always have. But I was willing to give you all I am, to spend forever to figure this out.

Miley Cyrus dropped "She's Coming" and I was still listening to "We Can't Stop," because baby, I don't want to.

Miley Cyrus divorced her husband and set out to recarve her path; to resculpt herself. She made herself into fresh art. She gave herself the time and space to restart.

I think I get her now. I think I know what I have to do if I ever want to be next to you *in* Malibu, or anywhere, but intoxicated, because I know I won't forget you.

> *"Baby, are you listening? Wondering where you've been all my life... I just started living."*[2]

Dream Lover

I've made love to visions of you so often that I can't get comfortable with another's hands touching me like you should.

Foreplay

Your mind turns me on more than any naked man could. Your thoughts keep me coming back for more, just like a filthy, intellectual whore.

The Humanity in Anatomy

You and I both bleed, but we don't pour from the same vein. You are piano wire fastened like a noose around a neck; worn like a necklace gifted from the lover who left you when she couldn't find herself. And I'm hemorrhaging from the years of beating myself black and blue; from punishing myself for thinking I could save people like you. I might've gotten an 'A' in biology, but I'm still learning... You cannot surgically reattach someone's head once it's been removed.

Writing on antidepressants makes my art fall flat—makes it feel like I've just suffered a heart attack.

My life has felt like one coronary arrest after another, living in a holding cell of my own doing, never believing I deserved more than concrete and metal bars, painkillers and sharp claws.

I am both the prisoner and the warden of the purgatory within my mind. I am cellmates and infirmary; the chef and the security. I don't feel safe inside me.

These pills should have been my bail money, my shock back into a regular rhythm.

My heart should be beating—I should feel alive and free.

So why do I feel like I'm doing solitary time again?

The Treadmill

I have been running for so long, trying to find the finish line, that I never realized it was the same scenery over and over that I kept running by.

Things won't ever change.

Omne Trium Perfectum

Three is a magic number... or so they say.
There's The Holy Trinity
And the number of years you promised it would take to be
with me.
I don't believe in you any more than I believe in religion now.
And I hate the number three.

Paranormal State

I won't lie. I've seen her ghost around the house. In dusty corners when sweeping up. In laundry when I shake it out. In the sheets when I turn them down. In my dinner when I heat it up. In the garden when I turn the soil. She's everywhere. And when I ask you if you've seen her too, you act as if she never lived here, as if she meant nothing to you. I can't live in this house, haunted by the ghost that wants to hurt *you*.

The Chopping Block

Trying so hard that I bend 'til I break,
I'm unsure if this fight is worth what's at stake.
Dreams have been shattered and promises torn apart,
My soul feels as empty as the hole in my heart.
My focus is blurry as tears flood my eyes,
Though I promised myself, "Tonight you won't cry."
No, they're no longer worth it; I've done all I can.
I've tried so hard to fix this, but I'm only human.
If time can erase what was done in the past,
Or if words can heal what couldn't last,
Then maybe someday there'll be light in my life,
But until then, this pain I feel will cut like a knife.

Scrapbooking

This is crazy. I cut my heart out of the picture and I'm still breathing. So, then I cut out my lungs and the nurse says there's still a chance of living. Art is what they call it when you write like *this*, but add the word "goodbye" and it's got a suicidal gist. The therapist on call says I have to see the bigger picture, but I threw out those scraps with my larynx when I finally stopped screaming. I asked the doctor what it takes for a vacation from my life for just one day. He handed me a bottle...

How many pills did he say I should take?

"Grandma, can you cut his ears?"

A childhood stuffed animal, now the size of my hand, is all the reminder I have that I was once happy... I fell asleep holding it, hoping I'd wake up happy again.

The Release of the Wedding Doves

You marry someone expecting safety, security. You never imagine that the one person you vowed "until death do us part" could hurt you so badly you can never look them in the eye again. But somehow "for better or worse" became worse and then worst. You look at yourself in the mirror and don't want to see your reflection anymore. Your eyes are dead. Your spirit is dead. Your heart is still beating but parts of you are surely dead. You look at the long line of undivorced family and don't want to be the one to break the chain. But some prisoners are wrongly convicted, and every caged bird still deserves its chance to sing. Some storms cannot be weathered, and I've cried a flood worth a million years.

> *I can't wait for the day my sobs become*
> *songs the free bird sings.*

Can I Take Batteries?

And she wrote "I'm exhausted by the energy it takes to hate myself,"[3] as if it's so hard to dislike what you see in the mirror... But the real energy is forcing yourself every time you pass a mirror to like the skin you're in. The skin that felt his hands on you, throwing you against a wall. The skin that got you called ugly throughout your school years. The skin that you tore apart hoping that seeing what was inside would make you feel alive. The skin that stretches over fat you just can't lose. The skin that was violated when you didn't give him what he wanted. It takes so much more energy to learn to love yourself than to just be able to walk past the mirror and never look at yourself again. And I'm already drained. None of the medication works to energize me. There is no adrenaline in my veins.

Electrical Shock

Someone please forget to pay the electric bill. Let the lights go out upstairs. I don't want to live with my thoughts anymore. Please, evict me from my nightmares.

Alanis Morissette

I'm dying in the living room and nobody can hear it,
A heart attack stomping out the last beat.
My heart isn't strong enough to fight through the disappointment
and the stress,
Of caring so much for others who couldn't care less.
I have thrown out the Chance cards from every Monopoly game,
Because I can't give them out anymore without feeling like
I am setting myself up for more shame.
When you hurt a good person you get off easy,
The first, second, third, eighteenth time,
But even the nicest of us have our limits.
But see, if I cut you off, stop you from leaching,
I'm afraid I'll bleed out and leave a mess for someone else to
be cleaning.
So, I silently force breaths under the weight of suffering,
To not burden anyone, to not cut them as deeply as they've
hurt me.
Tonight, it's too much and I'm sitting in the living room trying
to ignore it,
But I'm still dying...

Isn't that ironic?[4]

Repentance

Down on my knees, screaming, "Oh God,"
I have sins piled a mile high.
Saint Michael can use them as stairs on his way to Heaven's gate.
I drank the wine—alcohol flooding my body, my brain—
"I feel fine."
His blood in my body, my blood on his lips, as he sinks his
teeth into my shoulder,
Running his fingers down my spine... Vertebra by vertebra...
He's unhooking my bra.
Undressing me from the inside out; all the skeletons in my
closet become exposed,
And I'm trying on every one I own, to try to turn on the man
I want so deep he flows through my veins.
Unholy, unreligious, but, "Oh God, Praise Jesus!"
I see Heaven in his eyes, feel closest to His presence when he's
between my thighs.
His arms are all I need to save me in this lifetime.
I'm drowning but my body is on Cloud 9; unfaithful, my soul
is Hellbound.
Singing *Hallelujah* and hoping to be redeemed by releasing
years of lies in this confessional piece.
Forgive me Father, for I have sinned...
It's been fifteen years since my last confession...

Take the Plea Deal

I could've written a novel about you, but I wouldn't have known where to stop. But now I don't even think I could pick the pen up. My ability to write beautiful things was extinguished when you burned me. I'm nothing but ash now, leaving traces behind those who step all over me. I hope somehow the smell of igniter fluid on your clothes reminds you of your guilt every morning when you wake. And I hope one day it's too much for you to take. I hope you turn yourself in at the prison gates, and tell the warden how you killed the only love you'd ever made.

Watering Our Roots

Every teardrop like rain;
We all eventually fall...

One day returning to the Earth again.

You Need to Learn—Yesterday

I was taught that police wore their badge as a symbol of the oath
To serve and protect
I was taught
In case of an emergency, you call 9-1-1; the police will come
I was taught
They carry guns and handcuffs for bad *people,*
but you *don't have to fear*
Because I am white.
But African Americans and others of color were taught
Empty your hands, take off your hood, remain silent,
or you may die...
I learned that not all cops "serve and protect"
Equally and with fairness
I learned
Some people will never *feel safe calling the police to come*
I learned
I *may not have to fear, but...*
Have police learned
Skin color does not make someone a bad person?
Have they learned
Blue is not a skin color and skin color is a lifetime
Have they learned
You cannot just murder somebody
Because they were black.

No Heart Attacks

The Heart hasn't spoken to anyone in weeks. I call and text, but he won't open up. He's closed himself off and I can feel the tightness in my chest where not even blood can get through to him. I'd think I was having a heart attack, but I know Heart hasn't even been able to get out of bed, let alone throw a punch... The Left and Right Brain are arguing over how to handle the situation, but all I'm capable of hearing is the humming of another panic attack.

Taste Test

Do you remember what she tasted like? Her lips of cherry and her hips of spice...
The way her flavor changed at the door and between the sheets...
Tongue like ecstasy and thighs like cocaine...
She could keep you craving, keep you up for days...
Have you convinced yourself yet that we taste the same?
Or are you just using me to try to forget her taste?

Underdosed and Overwhelmed

The sun's gone down now—six Advil later and my head feels worse than when I woke up. I'll let this be my reminder that sometimes our drug of choice is not the right drug for our needs.

Naked Truth

Sometimes I wanna rip my hair out, rip my clothes off, pull my skin from the bones, pull the darkness from my soul. I don't want to exist as I am. I hate it here in this state, this "temple," this body I have to call home. I can stop paying the bills, but last I heard, eviction notices are still suspended in the midst of pandemic. Every day I get a little more stuck; get a little more frustrated. Maybe one day I'll move far away—so far away that when I rip my clothes off and pull skin from my bones, they'll think I'm beautiful and that I belong.

Because God knows, I have no purpose like this here...

Little Red Heart

Why were things so much easier when we were still talking like this?[5] Was it because we were strangers, or was it the complete opposite? Was it because we felt like we somehow knew each other...? Two strangers passing back and forth a blank notebook, filling pages, trying to get to know one another better with no expectations...
Learn more about each other than any lesson the teacher would test us on!
I think about it a lot—how *easy* it was! The feeling of knowing you and not just assuming I do, because we can't "talk" anymore without a fight ensuing.
I never imagined going back to a life without you in it,
And I know it was my choice, my pain that needs healing, but it doesn't mean I don't still miss you...
I do.

You're Not Difficult to Love

Spiders. Rodents. Shadows on walls.
It's hard to tell what's real anymore.
And closing your eyes hides the visions, but doesn't drown
out the noise.
Cover your ears. Count to ten. Box breathe until you begin to
feel real again.
   Who wants to be a square peg in a world of round holes?
Shut your mouth. Play pretend. Tell yourself the memories are
dreams instead.
     I'm here and I'll always remind you:
     Your worst days will soon be far behind you.
Hold on a little longer. Get out of your head. Reach for my
hand when we're lying in bed. I know it's hard. I know you're
tired of trying. But honey, please, stop crying. I promise, one
day you'll wake up and not feel like dying.
     You're safe now and I'll protect you,
         no matter how.

Bar, Numb, and Baileys

You make me feel fucking crazy. My stomach is sick from feeling like I'm always in a downward spiral with you. Where are the ups on this rollercoaster? I'm still trying to give you the benefit of the doubt, even when you don't deserve it. This must be a bad trip. The hundreds of chances I give you, like wasted tickets at this unfairground. And for what? So, we can end up right back here? No, that teddy bear won't make things alright this time. I don't want to hold the stuffed animal at night. I wanted *you*. This game we're playing feels like a scene from a horror movie. And no, I don't want to play a game, Jigsaw.[6] Is this a new record? Has anyone ever had a lower score? I feel stupid for ever letting you reach out to me again... Why do I keep crawling back? I don't want to be your slave anymore, doing tricks to be touched and praised. I'm done bending over backwards and putting myself in awkward positions for you to want to stay. I'm so tired of jumping through flaming hoops to impress you, just for you to ask me to jump higher the next day. I don't want to be the lady everyone stares at in the middle of a spotlight. I don't want the notoriety; it's time to take my life back. I am leaving this carnival, the monkeys, and the devil. Burn posters of my face down. I won't be coming back for your encore.

Is it Still a Slumber Party if You Don't Sleep?

It's getting harder to wake up again.
Because I can't fall asleep.
Because I can't stay asleep.
I stay up all night with my thoughts, until their fears become my own. We fight and sometimes I cry. It doesn't seem fair. It's funny how sleep evades me all night and I'm wide awake, but in the morning all my eyes, my mind, my body want to do is shut down. They're too young to be this tired.
It's sad that I can't remember what it felt like to enjoy the stream of sunlight dancing in my bed.

I Think I Dreamed You into Life

The universe must've put up one hell of a fight to bring our souls together. There's three years of difference, over 3,000 miles of distance, and yet it feels like the Holy Trinity is in charge at this very minute. The pull of my soul, the feeling that I "just know..." You complete a part of me I hadn't even known wasn't whole. Have I known you days or hours? A lifetime hidden by shadows?

The universe must've fought a bloody crusade just to make sure feelings like this get a name. To assure that you and I got to defy fate. That years of self-hate can be replaced. Someone like you could really help ease my pain.

The universe doesn't have to fight anymore. Your soul finally found me and beside you I'll stay.

Two bodies, one soul; my flame.

Remember to Breathe

Living without air...
It's a strange feeling—always gasping, grasping every last breath like it's your last breath. It's hard never knowing what will kill you first: your lungs or your brain. The doctors like treating the physical; they see the symptoms and see the progress. Steroids, stimulants, breathe it in and try to breathe out. Hands shake, mind races... What if it was invisible? What if the doctors made the mental worse?
Dying for air is ironic...
It's a strange feeling—always gasping, grasping every last breath like it's your last breath.

I'm Still Breathing

Breathing in masked oxygen. Breathing in peppermint-scented oxygen. Breathing in oxygen. I just have to remember I still have oxygen.

"What Do You Want?"[7]

The Notebook is not romantic.
The Notebook is not romantic.
The Notebook is not romantic.
Listen to me:
I wrote close to 300 letters and the person on the other end
received them.
Hasn't read them.
It didn't change anything.
It was just wasted trees and wasted time.
Writing how I felt just broke me.
The outcome was not what I hoped to get.

I wanted you.
But you never chose me.

All I Taste is Sour Now

Tonight, I walked into the kitchen without you and forgot
what I came in to eat because when I passed the window and
saw only myself in the reflection all I could think of was that
nothing would ever taste as sweet as your lips

3:33

I couldn't sleep again, but I couldn't go to bed. I promised I wouldn't sleep in here if it was without you, no matter how long. So, I'm sitting here with headphones on and trying to call you from the room next-door.

Please pick up.

Being Awake is a Nightmare

I don't want to sleep in this bed without you. So, I close my eyes, press them tight, the way I wish you held me tonight. Nothing would feel stranger or safer than your arms around me after all this time of separation. Nothing would make me happier than to wake up to your face.

I'll dream of you in every place that isn't my bed.

Still Standing Still

My feet hurt from running:
From my problems,
To you...
Ironically my feet hurt though I never move.

I only get anywhere in my head.

Who is Under the Mask?

I'm afraid of getting better because I spent so much of my life being bad that I don't know who I am without the doubts and depression; the anger and the need to please others to feel of value; the damage that came with being me.
Who am I underneath the mask I've worn all these years? Even I don't know. And that scares me.

Higher Education

Hating yourself is a learned behavior... You don't start life picking apart every aspect of yourself, creating a highlight reel of when you fell off your bike, dropped your toy in the toilet, ate all the cookies in a sleeve of thin mints... I don't want you to stop learning. Stay open. Try to remember who you were before failed tests, broken hearts, a number on a scale, or "falling off the wagon." Try to remember you are stardust and cosmos. You have gravity so strong, the planets all fight to be your neighbor, every moon bends the tides to you, and the sun is your star. You are an asteroid hurtling towards a new world. One day, people will make wishes on you as you soar through the atmosphere, more graceful than a ballerina and more forceful than a jet plane. And when you land you will leave your mark for all to remember that you existed, and here you lay, and "Oh, what a sight they were to see."

Learn to love yourself the way you love the night sky, because even in the dark the dimmest star shines bright.

Be Proud

"I kissed a girl and I liked it…" and I liked it more when she kissed me back. I felt alive for the first time when her lips met mine and I melted into her hands like a puddle of red wine—drunken, daydreaming, haphazardly falling. I felt more comfortable in my skin than I ever had before, but that was only until I felt her skin on mine. Wow! What a feeling! I felt more at ease in her arms than under an army command. Don't ask, don't tell… But I wanted the whole world to know because I loved her, heart and soul.

I kissed a girl and I liked it, but my family tore me out of family photos. They wouldn't invite me to Thanksgiving because seeing us together "ruins their appetite" and Lord knows that I can't stop them from devouring that feast. I wish I too could be thankful, but my mom still tells friends I'm just going through a phase. My friends became quiz-show hosts and detectives for the FBI. I've never felt more alone in a room of people I know. What does it feel like? Have we had sex? Who wears the pants? Who's on top? Have I always known I was straight?

I take a deep breath. I don't know what to say… Yes, I think I've always felt this way. But I tried really hard to suppress it, because it's uncomfortable when people act like this. It makes me feel defective for not being gay.

If you just cringed, felt uncomfortable, felt shocked, well…
Maybe it's because you realize how ridiculous that sounded.

Crescent

I've been waiting all day for you to come home. We both know we won't be sleeping tonight. When we lay in bed now, the moon is the only thing smiling.

Space Traveler

Cosmic bartender, fill my cup to the brim with moonshine.
I want to lose myself dancing tipsy on table tops with the stars.
I want to be weightless, effortless in my movements, wooing,
fooling the God of War into falling in love, want to watch him
rip the rings from Saturn to place on my finger. I want Venus
to drop her pride and beg me to stay. I want to float down the
Milky Way and dream of a view of the sun peering in from
my bedroom window, and wake up in the dark, quiet arms
of Pluto, to bathe in Neptune seas, remembering how awful
I once felt on Earth, and knowing...

I will never leave this space.

Revisiting the Conversation

Today, I realized I can't fix this mess I've become on my own.
I grew up so fast that I think I'm regressing now. Scotch-tape
and glue can't hold my broken pieces together, but I'm feeling
too small to hold the hammer and nails.
Today, I sent my heart out with its friends and let my brain
call a therapist.
They were right back then...

I can be fixed...
I'm going to heal...

Heart Needs a Rest

I muted the conversation to avoid you, but keep opening the app to see if you've sent anything. Why am I like this? It feels like Heart is five years old again, and running laps to prove he's not ready for a nap. All this jumping, racing, chaos... I want it to stop.

Left Brain hollers. He's the one that's had enough of you. He's the one that disciplines. He's the one that said "enough" and the ground shook. Heart stopped running then and sulked, resigned to going inside, lying down, closing his eyes. But... When Left Brain turns his back, Heart pulls out the phone— plays his game.

Right Brain comes and sits beside him, obstructing Left Brain's view. She knows this won't end well. She should be here to protect him, calmly tell him the things Left Brain is too violent to say, in such ways that the words stick and don't just sound like, "Blah blah blah anger, blah blah blah pain..." Right Brain keeps going MIA though; she can't stay anymore. See, she's run out of excuses for the bruises. One day, she promises she'll take Heart with her.

Go to sleep now. It's alright.

Heart puts the phone down.

Take it away and turn the damn thing off.

Right Brain shakes her head, knowing Heart will just wake up later and turn it into a treasure hunt; he won't rest until he's gotten the prize.

It's alright. Let it rest.

Please stop calling me...

My Heart needs its rest.

Passion Project

There's passion in your eyes, the way we kiss, between our thighs... But what I really want is to bring that same light and desire to your mind, to bring that passion to your spirit. I want to watch you soar above me in the sky. I want to motivate you; see you...

Become all I know you can be.

Modern Art

Make me your favorite piece of art—
Trace along my skin, outline every inch, paint me red;
Then pin me against the wall, keep me level with your eyes,
lose yourself in me.
Make sure no one else's hands ever touch me.
I trust you to keep me protected and secure.

Stairway to Heaven

Fireflies under moonlit skies and your eyes shining like diamonds, staring me down like a doe in headlights on a winding backroad, are the only light I see. I'm frightened not of the impact, the collision of bodies, but by the urge to jump head-first into the line of fire.
And then your hands are on my cheeks, my waist, my hips... I swear you must have eight of them, because I feel you everywhere. Collapsing into your embrace, I'm born again; rock my body with yours, find that sweet steady rhythm. Open me up to the constellations. Let us exhale into the night air and return to the stardust from which we came. Heaven is the only destination when your vessel is between my thighs.
I want you to love me.
Love me. Love me.
Or let me die.

I Wish You'd Been My Echo

I thought I was broken before you, thought I had nothing left.
But somehow, I found a lot to give; I emptied my heart from
my chest. I may have made you feel less crazy, but I was slowly
losing my own head.

Those things I said were things I longed
to hear from you instead...

Letter to You and Your New Old Love

I watched depression walk into the party and catch your attention. Watched her slither her way over to you. Watched her offer you another drink, another ten minutes, another chance to leave with her. I watched her whisper in your ear, I watched your eyes glaze over as she touched you where I touched you last night. I watched your hands tremble as you took hers and followed her out the door. The old adage of "comfort in the familiar;" the DJ was spinning it over and over all night long. I hate this song!

I watched you caress her, hold her, nestle into her beneath the blankets. I knew how you hated yourself for falling back into this pattern, but loving how familiar every sharp curve of her body felt. I knew this was coming because you canceled appointments, because they thought you'd need medication. I knew that her grasp was stronger on you than yours on her, and yet when your hand was around my neck, squeezing pressure, was it her you were thinking of fucking? You know, no one was jealous you took her home... except me. How sad is that? Jealousy...

I watched you make love to this demon instead of me for years. No treatment ever stuck for you because you preferred her pain to the ecstasy that could be obtained if you just went through a bit of a struggle day after day of breaking through rubble piled high like a castle of hurt that you've hidden away with no moat to approach you but throw me a rope because I swore I'd do anything to help keep you afloat and I would love you through "side effects" caused by the bottle of things that could show you that you're sick but that sick people get better but you choose suffering like it's all that matters and you know it's false advertising that this is "your whole life" and not just a chapter you must remember that there's no race to the finish line that you just have to get started but...

Depression is the old flame that just won't let you go and I can no longer ignore that I'm jealous of her and how you don't miss her birthday but mine slips your mind and how you know where she'll be time after time and yet you couldn't be there when I needed you to be mine and no "I love you" makes up for the infidelity of promises you'd get help and then finding you lying in bed with the monster knowing no phone call was made to find you a doctor and...

No.

No one was jealous that night you took her home again.

But if I'd gotten to her first, maybe you'd be okay.

Maybe you'd have stayed.

Maybe I will forgive you for making depression your wife instead, someday.

Bloodletting

I knew we were over the moment my heart stopped racing.
Love nor anger provoked my heart to beat for you anymore.
I have drained you from my veins for the last time, sucked out
your poison. There is no room left for you in me.

A Case for Happiness

I thought I knew hate when my first boyfriend wanted me to pick him over my sick father one week into "dating."
I thought I knew hate when my third boyfriend kept playing my emotions well after we were over.
I thought I knew hate when my fourth boyfriend left me via Facebook message with the audacity to still call me "babe" and ask if his decision was "right."
I thought I knew hate when my sixth boyfriend cheated on me and sprained my arm because I found out.
I thought I knew hate when my seventh boyfriend wouldn't work with me to bridge our distance after a year apart.
But when I found out how much time of my marriage I was blind...
I realized I didn't hate anyone but myself for believing someone else could make me happy.
I know now only I can make myself happy.

I will love me. Maybe not today. But soon.

To Whoever Needs to Hear This

This one is for you, the kids who had parents who:
Threw fists instead of baseballs and parties;
Raised voices instead of your spirits and you in their arms;
Loved you only when you were silent and unseen;
Tucked you in and then became the monster under your bed;
Took their walks without you and one day never came back.

This one is for you, the kids who:
Beat themselves black and blue to remember what it felt like
to be touched;
Carved into their skin to see if they really had the family blood;
Turned to alcohol and drugs to numb pain that wasn't easing;
Walked away from relationships before partners could find
one of the hundred reasons for leaving;
Thought of fulfilling prophecies of being "worthless" if doing
so would make their parents proud.

This one is for you, the kids who:
Walked into the office one day to start their journey of healing;
Talked to a dozen doctors and tried a dozen pills just to find
life a little more 'easy';
Now smile in photos with friends who became the family they
needed;
Now look into mirrors and like who they are seeing;
Found the strength to face the world when their protectors
made them think of leaving.

This one is for you;
To remind you to keep on living.

Unsolicited Hitmen Still Deserve Jail Time

You arrived late and don't know the story,
But there's a couple black people throwing a party.
You hear noise and know you "got the call."
How many 9-1-1 tapes sound like BBQs and baseball?
You walk on the scene unannounced,
Like this was a "surprise party"
In your honor, but...

Excuse me, Your Honor,
This is not okay!

He's spraying bullets like silly string,
Watching them fall like confetti.
What are you celebrating, Officer?
No one called you to commit a murder for hire.
You didn't "do your job."
They called you for help because
You wear your badge and uniform that should shout
"Trust me, I'm a cop."
But in what language does
"Serve and protect"
Translate into
"Racist hitman for hire?"
Look, we're not asking for insanity.
No, we're just asking

for humanity.

Your Ghosts

The distance has gotten so far and the time apart has gotten so long that I have gotten myself into thinking how if I was dead we could finally be together. If I died right now I would make it just into time to manifest beside you before you head to bed. But I would never feel your warmth and you would never feel my hands. With every movement you make while you are asleep you would just slip from beneath my fingertips. And I know deep down it would hurt you more to never hear my voice again than waiting one, maybe five more years, to hug you again.

I don't really want to become another
ghost for you anyway...

Customer Service

There will be no long hugs at airport gates and no heavy bags to carry. There will be no tearful "goodbyes" because "hellos" never started. I will use my money to build for *my* future again. I will burn letters I'll never send. I say I have left you, but can't seem to find me. I guess seven years is too far past the return policy. You will always have a part of me.

FAQ: How do you get yourself back after
giving yourself to someone else?

Two Days Down & Forever Yet to Come

Tonight is tough. Acid crept up my throat, threatening to break ten years of silence after forty-eight hours of trying to build silence between us. I know I'm the one who chose to leave but it was only because of you. See, there's only so much room for hurt before a person starts to believe they deserve it, and I was tired of believing someone I loved hated me so sincerely. And tonight, is tough. My mind turns with my stomach; both knot in bunny ears. I think I miss you more than ever, but I say that every time we're not together. I wish I could be dumb enough to call you, but I know that's not very clever. I know with time this will get easier and much simpler to do.
Tonight, is tough but I'm learning to be tougher without you. There are so many possibilities on the horizon if I just get through this night.
It's not worth it anymore. Unless...

Could we ever make things right?

Relapse

The blindness engulfs me as the rage sets in.
I want to scream; I pull my hair out like bobby pins.
I clench my fists, release, and let go...
My muscles are tense and my tears start to flow.
The darkness arrives, the horror begins,
Another night of "crazy"—the torture won't end.
The cold metal is whispering, calling my name.
I want to watch my blood fall like rain.
I scratch at my arms, bite my tongue, kick the door...
I know I'd promised you this wouldn't happen anymore...
I'm sorry.
I'm not okay yet.

Grave Feelings

I'm off my medication and nobody knows. I wanted to be able to cry again. I still felt so broken and I couldn't express it. I needed to let go. I think that was the last tree branch on the way down. There's nothing to grasp at now. I'm falling fast.

I think they'll find me underground.

I Can't Remember to Forget You

And I still think of you whenever I hear a line about a kitchen in a song, as if the words were being sung into my soul...

You're a Permanent Part of Me

And when the sun set tonight it tore down your pictures, wiped clean the slate. A new day was coming and we would not wake in the same bed. This is my last night surrounded by the scent of you before I wash these sheets, scrub you from my skin, and when the sun rises I'll open all the windows and let fresh air in. Wounds don't heal if you keep picking away protective covers, so I'll stop revisiting the knife you put in my back, won't look at myself in the mirror. Until the pain subsides and I begin to feel different, I'll go on long drives and blast all my "fuck you" music. Soon I'll forget the color of your eyes, but I'll remember your hands and how they left scars on me that I'll know for eternity.

System Error Code 573

Tonight, I couldn't sleep, so I checked and rechecked the shipping label on all the words I never sent you. Still unsure I packed it right, I went online to check the post office hours. I have so much I wish I'd told you. While online, I got the notion to Google that movie we watched right before we called it quits for first time, just to find a quote. Then, sidetracked, I watched the first twenty minutes of it as a silent track because normal people are sleeping. I stopped there to do a crazy thing and Googled that one actor's name. I stared at his face for so long my hate for him finally made no sense. If we ever talk again, if ever we are okay, I think I'm ready to finally watch that show with you. I should have done it back then.

I'm sorry and I miss you.

Night Terrors

I have been chasing sleep instead of dreams for a year because the last time I closed my eyes feels like a nightmare. What did I see that night that made it impossible for me to go back to sleep?

Nothing can be worse than reality.

Pick Me Last

I'm awful, gruesome, delirious, a freak...
I'm too far gone to be what you need.
You don't belong here; you don't deserve this hurt.
Don't make me the person you always put first.

The Promise

One day
I'll come home to you.
I promise to.
Don't wait up;
Sleep through the night.
But if you don't mind,
Leave on a light;
Keep the side door unlocked.
I won't be long;
You'll still be safe if you keep yourself open.
I'll come back,
And when I do I swear I'll protect you
Like I always do,
Love.
My love...
Always, my love.
Try not to miss me while I'm gone.
Remember,
You and I will always be one.

You Don't Have to Tell Me Twice

Kiss me, you say.
And I do...
Over and over and over again. I start at your lips, and don't stop until I've marked every exposed inch of skin. You never have to ask which side of these sheets is cooler, since we both know it's mine. Sleeping on your chest is my favorite position of all time.
Kiss me, you say.
And I do...
You don't ask; you command. All of me comes undone at the touch of your hand. You're one for undressing me from the inside first. Every word you speak to me sounds like verse, and I'm melting—I thought falling would hurt... But lying here beside you, I can say I'm a convert.
Kiss me, you say.
And I do...
Love has never felt this good.

Return to Insomnia Rivers

I thought their herbal remedies and medicines would help me
sleep;
Thought tuning you out,
And you,
And you,
And me would bring me some peace.
My head is spinning but I'm not sure I'm even thinking
anymore;
The thoughts of you,
And you,
And you,
And me don't even make sense at this degree of insanity.
It's been a month on their herbs and chemicals, and the only
thing I've seen isn't the inside of my eyelids or a crazy dream,
but of time passing by on the alarm clock.
It's been another week of waking up at 3 a.m. and watching
the sunrise from my deathbed;
Wondering...

Will I ever sleep again?

Now There's Three: Just a Dream for Me

Congratulations on your new adventure,
Your precious gift,
Your new role and title,
Your bundle of joy.
Forgive me if I don't stick around to talk,
To listen to your story,
To celebrate with you and your spouse,
To hear all your hopes and dreams.
But some of us are struggling with learning we may never go
on that adventure,
Receive that gift,
Gain that title,
Find that joy.
Some of us break down hearing your excitement,
And I'm sorry if it offended you when I extracted myself from
the celebration.
I didn't mean to ruin your party.

Stronger than the Storm

Head foggy,
Legs too heavy,
I think I can hear the ocean in this parking garage.
Hands sweaty,
Vision blurry,
It's just the sound of the blood crashing in waves inside my ears.
It feels like a hurricane.
I feel like I'm blowing away.
There are tsunamis inside me and I'd do anything to just spiral down the storm drain.
But I'm not drowning.
Not this time.

Tell Me About Your ~~Mother~~ Trouble

If I could speak to any famous person, dead or alive, it'd be Sigmund Freud. I'd tell him all about my family history until he regretted ever blaming mental disorders on the family tree. I'd tell him how I haven't felt alive since 2015, and that in 2020 I died and forgot to lie down. And then I'd ask him to interpret my dreams and explain what it means to never sleep but never be awake.

I'll Be the Son They Always Wanted

Heart beat so strong today. I wanted to be proud. But he frightened me so much when he began to get loud. Heart is beginning to show signs of his father's violent temper. I think I'm becoming too much Right Brain because I couldn't help but cry. When did I become so sensitive? Left Brain is going to have to beat me up, make me tougher, teach me how when in the wilderness to survive.

I Didn't Hate Myself with You

When I stopped writing beautiful words for you, it became painfully obvious how ugly I am without you in my view.

I couldn't see it then, but you gave me
the opportunity to see my potential.

A Drop in the Water

It's midnight.
I haven't closed my eyes yet.
They're heavy.
I'm sinking under their weight.
But I'm still wide awake.
It's so dark here; yet...
I think I'm the first person to see the bottom of the ocean
without any protection.

The Slowest Form of Suicide is Being Awake

The watch I wear tells me that in the last week I've only slept twenty-five hours. If I fall asleep now, with a pill on my tongue, some liquor in my veins, a pillow over my head, and your hands around my throat, I might get to sleep through the whole day...

Is that how making up for lost time works?

Pyromaniac

My brain is a house on fire, but instead of running out of the burning building, the Left and Right are fighting over who had the keys last, so they can get back in. My poor heart is going to suffocate in the smoke escaping my lungs, waiting for them to come in and rescue him.

Sleeping with Insomnia

Some nights I lie awake and want to cry.
Some nights I lie awake and write.
Tonight, I wrote six new pieces.
Tonight, I'll find no peace yet.
Sleepless nights are meant for lovers.
Sleepless nights turn the depressed into artists.
My bed felt empty without her...

Beneath the Covers

My back hurts from years of people picking up this book, but never caring enough to dust me off or read through the pages. Like summer reading—throw me down, fingers grazing along my spine, get what you need and go. But one day, body stiff from years of just sitting on a shelf, you cracked me open. You drew out a moan that started deep in my spine and escaped through my lips, a sound so strong it rattled the stars. I saw the universe explode in your touch. There was so much more to read in me, and somehow you couldn't put me down. You took me to bed, though we didn't sleep.

You are the only man to finish me.

Please

If I can't love myself, let me love you
In all the ways I ever wanted to love.
Let me bring a smile to your face,
Show you that time could never change
Anything I feel for you at the end of each day.
Let me bring you coffee in bed.
Show you how much I care
Beyond any words that can be said.
Let me be the one to call you sweetheart,
Be the one to call you to dinner,
Be the one to call you at work...
Let me show you that you're a masterpiece,
Worth disbelief and awe,
That there is beauty even in your flaws.
Let me love you in all the ways I wish I could
Love myself.

I won't even ask for you to love me back.

Lifecycles

It helps me to think we loved so hard because we knew our potential from a past life.
It helps me to think we tried so hard because we knew in another lifetime we would love again.

Oedipus

Your therapist asks you how your childhood was and you tell
her not to worry,
Because while your mother may have been emotionally absent
though physically there, your ex-girlfriend has a Jocasta
complex and she makes you feel safe—
She constantly reminds you that no one will be good enough
for her baby;
She tells you every day how proud of you she is, even if it's just
for getting out of bed.
You tell your therapist she was a great mother to your
hypothetical children.
You tell your therapist that you thought she would be
disappointed in you sleeping with women that meant nothing
but trying to move on...
Surprise! She wasn't, but swore if you found something serious
she would want to screen them.
You thought she was joking when she said she'd test your
future girlfriends,
Until 125 questions later you're stumped at #38 and starting
to doubt when your lowest point was.
Answer: when your parents got back together
Answer: when your ex-girlfriend died
No. Of course not that one. Before her.
Answer: When your ex-girlfriend left you and got married to
someone else
Yes. That one.
But you answer: *Now*

Because your therapist had the audacity to tell you you're in love with a woman who is only supplementing what you lacked from your birth mother;
Had the audacity to tell you her emotional closeness alone is not a relationship;
Had the audacity to tell you that what you two have right now is toxic and a sign that you both need help;
Had the audacity to say you need to have some time apart.
You thank the therapist for her time and politely tell her she doesn't know what she's talking about...
When you leave her office, you make a call
"I wish you could pick me up. I think I'm done with therapy now..."

The Eye of Our Storm

Last night I fell asleep to your thunderous snoring... their crashing blows somehow bringing me comfort. I could make those decibels sound like white noise. The chaos of your sleep is a sound I wish I had heard years ago. Maybe if I had, I'd be miles away in a foreign bed, instead of couples therapy for deciding whether to move on or stay wed. Or maybe I'd have fallen victim to our storm and wound up dead.

I guess some things we'll never know.
I think I'm still learning to be okay with that.

Lexapro

If I *can't* cry but I still *want* to...
Does that mean the medication is working *or not?*

Home Life: A Vintage Aesthetic

A cassette tape.
When you play it too many times you destroy it. The film rubs thin. It becomes loose. You need to keep it wound tight or it seeps through holes and cracks.
Listen!
You listen to it every day. Jam it into the mouth of metal. Turn it up to eleven. But you're not listening. You're fixing the car. Fixing the computer. Fixing everything but the cassette tape that's stripping mid-once favorite song.
Listen to me!
I've been talking to you for years.
I'm worn out.
You're eating me alive.

This is the Last Poem I Write for You

I'm tired of writing about you. Please, get out of my head. Our song has no music. Our relationship is dead. Please, let me go. Please, sleep in your own bed. I want to be able to move on now. I'm tired of always waiting for you instead.

Lesson for The Heart

Heart has been holed up alone in a room with Left Brain for five days now. This isn't at all what he thought homeschooling would look like. There's not enough blood pumping through his veins to take down notes fast enough without cramping. They're only averaging about two a day, but the material is overwhelming.

Love, loss, regret and mistakes, following dreams but only if they're rationally sound... The easiest so far was 'say no to drugs.' Left Brain is so smart!

Left Brain fires off another.

Lesson number ten: You can trust a brain or a gut, but never a heart.

Heart raises his eyebrows first, then his hand. He can't believe what he's just heard. That can't be right. Never trust a heart? But everyone should follow their heart— it's their passion. Left Brain has to be smart to believe that, too...

Why not?

Left Brain explains that hearts are too emotional, too involved and "connected" to everything else; afraid to hurt feelings or make hard decisions; it has a pulse and one mistake could kill it. He says hearts can't be trusted when something as mundane as eating too much cheese could stop them from beating, but even knowing that never stops them from building up plaque instead of muscle! He tells Heart that guts sustain energy and immunity. He tells him brains are the smarts, intelligence—they hold knowledge and can assess situations, like… whether that was in fact too much cheese in one sitting.

Heart is confused (just more ammunition for Left Brain to prove Heart's not as smart as he thinks) and he asks why, if brains are so smart, why he and Right Brain can't ever agree.

Left Brain looks down and sighs.

Because the two halves aren't equal. There's a reason for the line down the middle. He says the Right is always too attached to the heart—rationalizing evades her, and she makes too many "oopsies" in one day. She likes to create scenarios in her head that have no reason or validity, instead of just seeing the bigger picture for what it truly is. She focuses on details and has grand expectations, and when those expectations fall short, she ends up disappointed and gets so upset she can't function properly—can't sustain a body.

Left Brain stands proudly as he says that only Left Brains gather the facts and assure that sanity always remains. He is order and control. He is brain and brawn. He grows daily. That's why he's the teacher—Heart's new leader.

Write this down.

Heart picks up his pen and writes:

Lesson eleven: Stop questioning your logic because of your feelings. Sadness won't make a fact lose its meaning.

"Do You Want to Play a Game?"

Where is the crazy glue?
We've been at this for hours,
Trying to fix broken pieces, like Alice didn't just shatter the looking glass and expect us not to find out.
Do you think if we put it back together anyone will notice?
How looking at our reflection would make it appear that we failed, when the images of you and me are displayed incorrectly
Because there's no way your hands are around my neck, no way my nose is that high up in the air, no way you're crying on the floor, no way I'm walking out.

The picture on the box looked nothing like this when we bought it...

Maybe the pieces don't belong. Maybe we started two different puzzles. Maybe you and I are not the solution, but maybe we're the problem.
And breaking off the knobs of pieces just leaves us with more holes...
Aren't you tired, like me, of looking like we do—empty and hungry, waiting to feel full
Of light, of life, of love, of [you]?

If we smash the broken parts of us a little more, no one will even know how we were supposed to look... But will we remember?

How your key fit my lock, how my light fed your soul, how
sharing small spaces beat sleeping alone,
And how we once made a home in each other's pocket, never
to be too far from the ability to feel hands slip in and touch us,
Hands that once felt welcoming and filled with comfort, that
once felt right,
That once with one touch made us feel alive...
We are still the same people
So why don't we make sense when laid bare on the table?
How many corner pieces got cut because we were too tired
now to even try to make us stable?

> *I just want the solution to our puzzle...*
> *I want to like the image staring back at me.*

I'm No Longer Loaning Myself to Those Who Cannot Pay

I hurt myself, expecting the effort I put into others to be returned—the time, the energy, the kindness. It wasn't even about the finances! But God, if I had gotten back even one dollar for every time I jumped through a hoop, only to come out on the other side lonelier, my student debt wouldn't exist. I'm no longer giving myself to those who don't respect me. I'm going to become someone people miss instead.

I'll Pay

Marked me, used me, like ink you bleed into skin,
Left to fulfill you until every outline was colored in.
Command my presence, unwrap me like a birthday present,
For there's no time better than when you're "bored" to forget
hesitance.
Play with me when no better option is around, and hate me
when I'm "cruel,"
Then walk away proud you've had it all and let me feel a fool.
To be so close to letting you in, so close you were at my door,
Just to realize you didn't want me for me, that you just wanted
"more."
Do you think you know anything about me because you saw
me without clothes?
The parts of me that matter you will never know
Because honestly, you don't deserve my soul.

You can't afford this.
& I'm not cheap.

Participation Trophy

I used to say at the outcome of our fights that "you win."
That you must not have wanted me around anymore. And ever so loyal to you, with my tail between my legs, I'd crawl into the doghouse to lay.
That you were always testing the waters to see how much sludge I'd swim through for you, and Lord knows how weak my heart has become from overuse.
That you spewed nothing but venomous toxicity into the air around us, and I have felt how diseased my lungs have become from breathing for you when life got too tough.
You always got what you wanted. You never had to try for anything. You could just glide by on having been present.
Well, not today. Today you lost.
Because when you finally pushed me away, you lost the one person who had always wanted to stay.

You can't get a participation trophy for a one player game.

Inanimusia

My stomach growls though I just ate.
I guess my brain finally reached its lowest point and its hunger
for more must be fed.

Uninviting Suffering

You are a mixer of rainstorms before rainbows and a long winter of summer dreams. You've blended with the visions of things you were once too young to have seen. It has made you the fixer of broken people, places, and things; because you know many people also suffer, and you've personally held hands with suffering.

He knows your favorite color is black and you hate the sound of your own name. He knows how you checked out of the party tonight even before you came. He watches as you stand in the kitchen looking for a place to get away. He watches you stare at people who already found the mixer that fixes their mood today. He knows how you want to be the drink that quenches another's thirst, but whispers in your ear, "Remember, you're a poison in broken glass first."

You are a mixer of rainbows after rainstorms, and a summer dream after a long winter. You've blended with the visions of things you were once too young to have witnessed. Yes, many people suffer, and you've held hands with suffering. But you are stronger now, regained your self-control... It is okay for you to now let him go. Let me remind you that...

You were a mixer, but now you're neat. You don't need to hide at parties waiting for someone new to meet. Fill your cup first and make it straight. Don't become anyone else's cocktail tonight.

Not Dead Yet

There's an old wives' tale that states if you try giving CPR to a conscious, breathing person you can kill them... I know it's not true, but it won't stop me from telling you:
No matter how dead I am inside, I need you to stop trying to breathe life in me; stop exhaling your lies in me; stop wasting your time and your oxygen on me...
Stop.
You're hurting me.
Take your hands off me.
I don't want you near me.
Yes, losing you may kill me,
But
I don't need you to save me.
> *My heart won't beat for you anymore...*

Rainbows and Butterfly Dreams

Watching you walk down the aisle,
I had always expected you in a tuxedo;
I had never expected you to exist;
I had always expected to be full of life in this moment;
I had never expected my hands, like crepe paper, to shake as
they touched you.
I've woken up to screams again; my screams.
I'm old, my memory is going, I'm dying.
I try to remember...
I had always only ever wanted one title;
I had never expected to be a mother;
I had always wanted to name you Bodhi;
I had never even gotten Cecilia.
You don't exist, son; you never even surprised me as a daughter.
Turns out, some women just aren't born to become mothers.
                    I'm still trying to come to terms with that...

Morning Mantra

I woke up with nothing but the sheets on my skin
Walked into the kitchen and for the first time appreciated the
patter of my bare feet on the tile floor
Because you hated feet, and so socks were always worn.
This room was once the entire house to us two lovers;
We talked here, ate here, fought here, slept here...
(Yes, I said "sleeping," but our eyes weren't shut...)
But I made my coffee strong and used it to become stronger.
I'm a woman to be feared because I finally woke up knowing
you didn't deserve me any longer.
I have nothing left to give you that you haven't already taken
from me
And I won't make plans anymore that require "your satisfaction,
guaranteed."
I went back to bed without feel guilty...
Body naked, hot coffee in my veins, "I'm still alive" pulsing in
my brain, and a promise to myself that...
This time it won't take alcohol for me to try forgetting your
name.
This time I know, with enough time, I'll be okay.

It's Not You, It's Me

I wish you'd told me I was fat, called me a slew of names that made even a boxing match look peaceful in comparison to the weapons used in your attack.

I wish you'd cheated on me, hurt me in a way that made me leave you with the whore you swore you didn't know two days ago despite the fact that I had you first.

I wish you'd hit me, left a few bruises that would remind me when I stretched the next morning that love shouldn't hurt and I'd just keep going without you.

I wish you'd choked me out, left me unconscious long enough to forget you for days until every memory of us began to fade.

I wish you'd said you didn't love me anymore, broke my heart instead of my soul when you walked out the door and stopped picking up your phone.

I wish you'd made it easier over the years to hate you, but you were the best and I drove you away and it sucks so much that I still think of you every time it rains...

Tears and showers both look a lot like rain...

My Encore

I had to let you go to hold on to me, and now I'll write poems
for you that you'll never read. You may have broken my heart,
but you won't ever break *me*.

> *I'm going to make my dreams come true and*
> *I don't need you to become all I'm yet to be.*

P.S.

I said I wouldn't write for you anymore, but you're the only one who cuts me so deep at my core. I can't count high enough to let you know how many times I've hated parts of myself because I always cave in to you. And the worst part? Had I felt like I could talk to you, you'd know I learned why in my session the other day. But now all I want to do is find the corner of the earth farthest away from you. Sometimes when I'm alone, I can still remind myself that you don't get to make me feel anything I don't want to. Sometimes when I'm alone I wonder if I finally hate *you*.

I sometimes hope you hate me too... Then I'd know why you make me feel like you do.

I Can't Even Be Angry at You on Paper

I said I wouldn't write for you again, so...
Why am I here?
Maybe it's because it's a safe space to get my thoughts out about you right now, since I'm not yet done venting.
Or maybe it's because no matter how much I feel disappointment, your love was like a salving ointment,
And you made me feel beautiful and it's okay that nothing flows to end that statement with a rhyme because I need you to know that.
I need you to know that I mean it.
You made me feel beautiful. Even on the days where I hated myself...
Wanted to smash every mirror...
I wish when I reflected on our past, there'd be a sign on the glass that read "objects are nearer."
Because at the end of the day,
Four thousand miles is quite the distance, and some days with you felt like a test of resistance,
But no matter the struggle... I always wanted you closer.
You were my other half;
You were my sense of composure.
I don't know if I can do life without you and...
Maybe I wrote this because I just needed to get it off my chest before putting us to rest...

Grounds for Divorce

When they ask you on what grounds you petition for divorce, remember all the times I caused you emotional and mental distress. Try not to remember how the doctors all tried to convince you to stay; how they told you I could get better with time. Try not to remember the vows that unite us through sickness and in health. Remember how I'm always sick and how that was not part of the plan when we vowed "until death do us part." I'm sorry I'm too strong even at my weakest I postpone death. But don't let that strength deter you from telling the lawyer the truth, how living with me living with BPD has been the death of me. Tell them...

1. How I always need my space. How I like to be alone. How when I work in the office I don't like to be approached. How all my hobbies are solo art. How if I text you I expect a response. How if I call you and you don't answer I'll ignore your call back. How when you're online with your friends I'm imagining how much happier you are without me. How when you offer to run errands alone I wonder if you are trying to get away from me. How I will lock myself away with a sign on the door to not approach but still expect you to broach the fortress and try to rescue me from myself.

2. How I'll hate you for not trying, and love you only for a while, while my "thank you" is still fresh. How when you walk away to let me rest, I'll hold you with disdain for not choosing to stay and assure I'm okay. How I make friends so easily; how I give them my all, but never get back what I put out and lose friends just as easily. How I have a history of week-long relationships because commitment is scary, but I don't want

anyone else to leave me. How black and white are ways of life and not just colors, and grey matter makes up my brain but it doesn't work right.

3. How I will flaunt myself under your nose, dangle myself just out of reach, only to tell you I'll only go to bed with you if the lights are off. How I can't ever decide what I want to do with my life, but I am nothing without a title at the end of my name. How I sometimes wish I was dead, but know how important I am to others. How I just can't make heads or tails of myself, even if both sides were equal.

4. How others call me "cool" for always picking "dare"—for "living on the edge." How I put the pedal to the metal even though I know it scares you when I drive. How my vices are never healthy; there are cigarettes hidden throughout the apartment like others stash money and chocolate. How I've been afraid to enter a casino because adrenaline is my favorite hormone and I wouldn't know when to quit.

5. How I have scars inside far worse than those visible on my skin. How my skin was a canvas painted only in red, but my favorite art form was always sculpting. How I've spent so much time collecting ways to die I could write a book on the topic. How I learned which states have the "right to die." How I wrote a poem in the name of Dr. Kevorkian. How even my therapist is unsure I'll ever quit carving all the times I've hated myself into my skin.

6. How I'm always "in a mood." How minor irritability flips to explosive anger within moments when you breathe too close to my skin. How if you make me repeat myself or make asinine

noises I am ready to scream like you murdered my mom. How I can never pinpoint my trigger but expect you to know better. How moments after an outburst I'm in tears, apologizing and spewing all my fears. How I will hate myself more than I ever hate you. How I'm an emotional rollercoaster at Action Park and I never learned how to control the speed. How happiness comes off as manic and some days, just using my inhaler is enough to make me appear like I'm on speed.

7. How I'll never make a decision on what to do, but I will always know what I don't want to do. How I have a million and one game plans and no concrete finish line. How I lost myself when I lost my job. How I could be knee-deep in an archaeological dig and still be bored because I haven't found anything exciting to me. How I could receive a birthday card from every family member I know and still feel unloved. How you could buy me flowers every day and I'll just sit and watch them decay. How I'm empty even when my emotions are overflowing. How I can't recall what it's like to be happy.

8. How when we take pictures you hate how you look so we take another, but I don't even recognize it's me beside you. How I always feel like friends are hiding that they hate me, and people who hardly know me just wish I would disappear. How every post I make I feel others roll their eyes. How when I look down at my feet some nights, they scare me because I don't feel like they're mine. How dissociation scares me, but is the most pleasant experience—to have time away from *me*.

So, when the lawyer asks you why you're looking to get a divorce... Tell them I'm crazy. Tell them you also just want to get away from me.

The Left is Right and The Right is Wrong
Part 4 (Heart's Surgery)

The Heart has been tinkering in his room. A wire seems loose or maybe too tight. Pieces lie where they don't belong. Maybe if he had become a doctor he would've made his parents proud...

The Left and The Right haven't bothered him in days because they no longer know what to say. The Left has made it clear this time. The Heart didn't even tremble at the sound of his voice when he said it was over. The Right didn't even put up a fight. She's like live TV on mute; no one in the house wants to hear her anymore, but they'll watch and make assumptions—try to read lips when hers are sealed and then spread rumors about what she means.

The Heart laces in the last stitch like embroidery. He's going to be okay. He's been told "scar tissue is thicker" and he hopes he grows the thickest of skins. He's done hurting and can't remove any more limbs. He looks down at every piece he has removed, pieces that were touched by you, and wonders how he is still beating. The Heart sees the carnage and finally understands that The Left is right... This was no good.

The Heart is ready to move on.

Footnotes

1 *Inspired by <u>Alice in Wonderland</u> by Lewis Carroll*
2 *Lyrics from "Adore You" by Miley Cyrus*
3 *Inspired in response to a poem in <u>Home Body</u> by Rupi Kaur*
4 *Inspired by "Ironic" by Alanis Morissette*
5 *A reference to the Tumblr messaging service*
6 *A reference to Jigsaw's quote in <u>Saw</u>*
7 *A reference to Noah's monologue in <u>The Notebook</u>*

Author's Note

I started this book with the most important note already written, a message to you, reader. The most important thing I can say is thank you. Even if you didn't like what you read, you still picked up this book—you (likely) contributed to my sales or someone you know did. That already means a ton!

However, there is more I want to say.

I know some of the material in both *Divorce of the Left & Right* and in its predecessor, *Conversations from the Left, Right, & Heart* can get heavy. I know to some it could be an emotional trigger (please, put this book down if you are struggling through it). My purpose was never and is never to offend or add to emotional hardships, and I hope I have not. My hope in writing these books was and always will be trying to connect to people; to let them know that whatever they might be feeling, there are words for it after all, and that you are not alone. You are never alone, and it is never too late to ask for help, whether it be from a loved one, a trusted teacher/spiritual leader, or a medical professional. And I want to assure my readers that while the emotions you read here are real and they are raw, I am okay, and I greatly appreciate messages asking such. I hope you're all taking care of yourselves, too; and if you ever *need* someone to talk to, please dial 1-800-273-8255.

2020 was a hard year. 2021 wasn't much better. But every day is a new opportunity—24 hours to do anything you set your mind to; to change your life; to turn things around. Seize that moment. Build your dreams. Chase them. I want you all to succeed and be happy.

Thank you again for listening to more of my late-night thoughts, word-vomit and musings. You are my reason to write.

—Me ♡

If you'd like to read more or interact with me:

Instagram   **Facebook**
@amsgpoet   https://www.facebook.com/amsgpoet